For Carrie Bell, my queen in the sky.

Published by The Blackberry Preserve
Montgomery, AL & Washington, DC
www.theblackberrypreserve.com

Designer: Frederick James Pellum III, of
Passion Energy Lighthouse, LLC
Illustrator: Tiffany Tafari Housey
Consultant: Arlisha Norwood
Page 3 photo courtesy: Michael Cairns
Page 28 photo courtesy: Darren Freeman

ISBN-13: 978-0615938707
ISBN-10: 0615938701

This heirloom belongs to Queen

_____

A rule for my reign:
If I honor and serve others, others will honor and serve me.

A Note Especially for You:

As a Miss America, it has been my honor to serve as America's Queen. My dream as a child was to one day become a woman recognized and respected for her talent, intellect, poise, professionalism and beauty. I now understand that is the deeply held dream of so many girls. "Queen Like Me" profoundly illustrates the direct correlation between strong queens of the past who defied opposition and lived courageously with our present potential to achieve greatness on stages, in classrooms, in sports, and wherever else we choose to tap into our majesty. Our girls should embrace and embody this legacy in all that they do.

The undisputed "Queen of Television & Media," Oprah Winfrey once advised the following words of empowerment, "Think like a queen. A queen is not afraid to fail. Failure is another stepping stone to greatness."

My goal is to equip our girls to esteem themselves beyond life's challenges and failures as demonstrated by the illustrious queens throughout this book. As you flip through these pages, I invite you to allow your imagination to take you to a time and space where YOU make all of the rules. YOU are worthy, valuable and beautiful. YOU are queen.

Yours Truly,
Ericka Dunlap, Miss America 2004

Hatshepsut was a regal woman …who ruled Egypt as a king!
She built temples and so many beautiful things.

No one could tell her girls couldn't be in charge.
Believing in herself is how she ruled a kingdom so large.

She controlled the whole land for over 20 years, you see.

Indeed, indeed, she was a queen
…like me!

Now, there was also a beautiful girl named Tiye.
She came from a rich and noble family.

When she grew up, she became a Great Royal Wife.
So smart, she advised mighty pharaohs and courts all of her life.

She was the first to have her name placed on official acts, you see.

Indeed, indeed, she was a queen
...like me!

No one can ever forget Nefertiti's lovely and divine brown face.
Her bust sits in a museum and STILL draws millions of people
from all over the place!

Everyone admires her blue headpiece, so stylish, yet odd.
She and her husband changed how the world would see God.

She believed in only one Supreme Being, you see.

Indeed, indeed, she was a queen
...like me!

O how Nefertari was adored by Ramses 2 (Two)!
He built her the most magnificent and famous tomb.

Statues made in her imperial honor are 33 feet high!
She wore gold headdresses and shimmering bracelets
today's money can't buy.

Ramses wrote that the sun shines for his beloved, you see.

Indeed, indeed, she was a queen
...like me!

The story of Sheba is known by many,
including Christians, Muslims and Jews.
On her way to meet King Solomon she
brought incense, spices and jewels.

She arrived from Ethiopia, the origin of the entire human race.
The king offered gifts, as he was delighted by her
brilliance, charm and grace.

She asked many questions to enrich her wisdom, you see.

Indeed, indeed, she was a queen
...like me!

Nzinga was a fierce leader with a whole army under her command.
She battled the Portuguese to keep them from taking her land.

They sought to capture her people and make them slaves.
But Nzinga had none of it. She was clever, fearless and brave!

She won the battle and protected her territory, you see.

Indeed, indeed, she was a queen
...like me!

Anna Jai Kingsley had been a princess,
but was kidnapped from Africa's west coast.
She was enslaved in Florida after being bought and sold.

But she studied business and labor so this wouldn't be the case for long.
She secured her freedom and owned an enormous farm.

She became rich and highly respected, you see.

Indeed, indeed, she was a queen
...like me!

The ones who came before created a path as guiding lights.
Just think of Mother Tubman, Ida Wells, and Dorothy Irene Height!

We must always recall Harriet Jacobs,
Nannie Helen Burroughs, and Anna Cooper too!
Ah! This world just wouldn't be the same without Mary McLeod Bethune.

Harriet Tubman

Ida Wells

Anna Cooper

Mary Bethune

Remember freedom fighters Assatta,
Rosa Parks, and, of course, Fannie Lou!
Remember dazzlers Diahann Carroll, Cecily Tyson,
and Phylicia Rashad just to name a few!

The story isn't complete without Coretta Scott King,
Ella Baker, or Ruby Dee.
Surely, Shirley Chisholm opened doors
for First Lady Obama, you see.

Indeed, indeed, all of them are queens
…like me

Assata Shakur

Rosa Parks

Coretta Scott King

Michelle Obama

Everybody gazes at Grandmama strutting
in church with her classy suit and hat.
She can even cook aaaaand shoulder-hold
the phone when she and her friends chat!

I love the way Mama hugs me, squeezes my cheeks
and kisses my head,
the way she makes me do my school work and
say my prayers before heading off to bed.

I make sure to thank God every night for them, you see.

Indeed, indeed, they are queens
...like me!

I smile thinking of all the amazing things that I can do.
Honey, it may take more than a million years for me to even tell you!

I can run. I can jump. I can dance. I can do my own pretty hair.
I can do math and I read so much that my thoughts go super high in the air!

It's in my genes! Just look at all the magnificent women
and girls in my family tree.

Indeed, indeed, they are queens
...like me!

Scroll of My Favorite Queens:

_____

_____

_____

_____

_____

_____

About The Author:

"...imits on our potential evaporate when we can look in the mirror and like what we SEE."

Kimberly Brown is an assistant professor of history at Alabama [Sta]te University. Researching 20th century African American women [and] the politics of beauty, she earned a doctoral degree in United States [hist]ory at Howard University. She has worked in Washington D.C. as a [Gold]man Sachs Multicultural Fellow at the Smithsonian Institution [Nat]ional Museum of American History. There, Dr. Brown served in the [dep]artment of public programming in which she facilitated "Join the [Stu]dent Sit-Ins," an interactive educational series which commem[ora]tes the Greensboro Lunch Counter Demonstrations of 1960 and [teac]hes the public about non-violent direct-action training strategies. [She] is a former Miss Florida A&M University, Miss Black Alabama, host [of] the Miss Africa USA Pageant and current orientation manager for [the] Miss Black USA Pageant and Scholarship Organization. Her insight [as an] analyst of aesthetics and expertise as a historian often intersect [to il]luminate the complex contours and meanings of women's images [in A]merica. This multi-dimensional work was captured in "Groomed [for] Greatness," an exhibit curated by Dr. Brown and displayed for three [yea]rs at the Mary McLeod Bethune Council House National Historic [Site] (National Park Service). Most importantly, Dr. Kimberly Brown [inn]ovatively applies her specialization as a scholar to develop lifestyle [met]rics to assist women and girls with minimizing the influence of [imp]osed standards, but rather cultivating positive self-identities for [the]mselves. She advocates history education as the optimum guide for [self]-determination and personal development and travels extensively [to f]ulfill this mission. Dr. Brown often shares, "Limits on our potential [eva]porate when we can look in the mirror and like what we see."

CPSIA information can be obtained
at www.ICGtesting.com
Printed in the USA
LVHW071143081118
596412LV00002B/25/P